IN THE DOG HOUSE

Wanda John-Kehewin

IN the DOG HOUSE

Talonbooks

Talonbooks
P.O. Box 2076, Vancouver, British Columbia, Canada V6B 3S3
www.talonbooks.com

Typeset in Arno
Printed and bound in Canada on 100% post-consumer recycled paper
Cover illustrations by Jessica Mullen (www.jessicamullen.com) Creative Commons License 2.0
Cover and interior designed by Typesmith

First printing: 2013

The publisher gratefully acknowledges the financial support of the Canada Council for the Arts, the Government of Canada through the Canada Book Fund, and the Province of British Columbia through the British Columbia Arts Council and the Book Publishing Tax Credit for our publishing activities.

LIBRARY AND ARCHIVES CANADA CATALOGUING IN PUBLICATION

John-Kehewin, Wanda, 1971–
In the dog house / Wanda John-Kehewin.

Poems.
Also issued in electronic format.
ISBN 978-0-88922-749-1

I. Title.

PS8619.O4455I5 2013 C811'.6 C2013-900216-2

For my children

CONTENTS

PREFACE

In the Dog House is for those who are First Nations, who will understand the pain and loss expressed here. It is also for those who wish to understand the effects of colonization on a personal level, from the perspective of a First Nations woman. With raw honesty, these poems address the loss of culture and the search for ways to adapt, found through reflection and stumbling upon "right" answers. Poems collected here discuss taboo topics like alcohol addiction, abandonment, religion, and sexual abuse; what it is like to try to understand all these experiences as part of the creative-writing process; and what freedom comes when we finally give up the shame and stigma.

In the Dog House is a healing journey of sorts, a way to stand in my truth, and a way to give others, like my mother, a voice. It is about the love of Mother Nature and the quest for love even though I don't understand what love is: can anyone really describe a normal kind of love or a love so perfect without ever having had an example?

This book touches on everything in my being as a First Nations woman searching for the truth and for a way to be set free from the past. The inspiration to write has been my children and the children who have lost one parent or both. As a result, *In the Dog House* provides a way to delve into and understand another's pain so the abandonment is no longer personal, but a life lesson in strength and understanding, and in leaving space for personal growth for oneself and for future generations. Other influences are friends whose stories are so like my own that I can find the strength to be raw and honest and know I am not alone and that we relate to other human beings through pain, suffering, and loss.

– WANDA JOHN-KEHEWIN

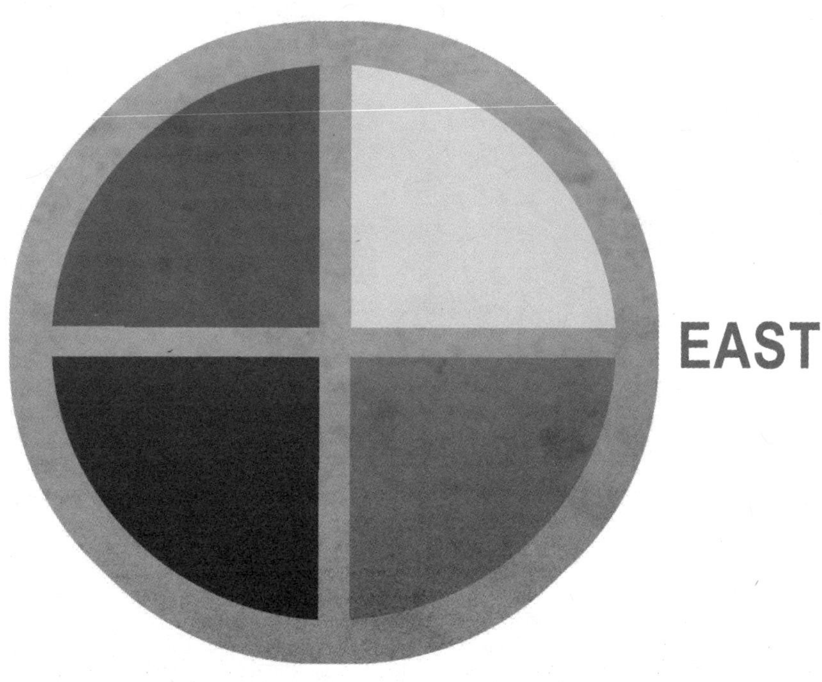
EAST

RED WARRIOR WOMAN

Slow down.
Take a breath –
It hasn't even begun.
I've watched your struggle
in a world not of your making.
I've watched your tears fall,
and make the ground shake.
I've heard your solitary cries
desperate for understanding.
I have felt your suffering vibrate
on a starless night when you
want to give up and yet
you know you are not finished.
Let go of the past and use it to teach.
Discover your culture and use it to find …
Stop questing for love that is not
worth a single stone upon the altar
of the ancestors and souls of the lost.
Let go of ego and just be …
Stop being afraid of judgment.
Be what you were destined to be.

STRAWBERRY JAM

The smell of strawberry jam wafts through the air
and brings her back to her kokum's♥ kitchen ...
The sunlight pushing its way through the door, reaching.
The soft, cool wind bringing new smells and hope,
while the birds sing and call out to old friends
to ask where they each spent the winter ...
The grass just sprouting green and the old melting
into the damp, fresh earth renewing itself ...
The soft, freshly made bannock slathered in margarine and jam
melts in her mouth ...
and the sweetened, warm tea slides down her desperate throat.

She sees the sun reaching farther inside as it touches her kokum's moccasin
that is gently tapping on the floor with a soft *tshhht tshhht* sound
and hears her laboured breathing, in and out, after cooking and cleaning,
making the house smell like a pine-tree grove and bakery ...
The dogs let out yelps and yips as if to tell each other
that they will no longer be cold because the taste of spring just touched
their hungry tongues and brought peace and warmth,
and that Kokum will be giving them leftovers soon.

Watching her little brother gobble bannock
brings a tightness to her throat
in a way that she can't explain because Mom left again
and time didn't stop ...
Neither did the smell of strawberry jam and bannock ...

♥ Kokum: Cree for "grandmother."

BiRth

The harsh light leaves me cold
and solitary, confined in my mind,
wanting for a mother never there.
Here I am with my soul awakening,
being reconstructed into everything
the past was not or ever could hold,
as my daughter creates her way out.
Two days later, the sweetest pain –
excruciating, beautiful, magical.
The longest memory filled with truth
when I see her tiny, angry, red face
and she screams her first complaint
and I let her feel her feelings.
She was afraid, the moment she entered
the earth's harsh light.
But she is a force to be heard, prayed for,
loved, and planted in untainted soil.
Wanting to get her an immunization
from pertussis, chicken pox,
and colonization.
I look at her face today, almost nineteen.
She still gets her chocolate milk
and has a puppy and a favourite blankie
although she would never tell you that.
She still feels what she feels, without suppression,
but I still never found the colonization shot …

THE WARRIOR COMES OUT

The warrior comes out
when an Indian is backed
into a corner.
They will
claw for freedom,
claw for something
good.
They will
try, try, try again
and again to recover.
They will
cry and question why
or die trying.
They will
accept it,
walk around it,
and even through it.
Resilience passed on
from the ancestors,
paving the way
back home
through words,
passed on through
oral tradition,
through eyes,
through ears,
that have heard lies,
through the heart
that continues to love,

through soul
that refuses to kneel,
and leads you through
the darkness,
searching for the light,
together,
always together –
"It is a long way home
but not impossible,"
they say as they sigh
and light the sage
of good thoughts
and intentions
and pray for
self-pronounced
enemies,
and give thanks
that we have survived
thus far
and that our children
are one step better
than we were raised.
Without the teachings,
humility
respect
faith
love
kinship
thankfulness
sharing
prayers
our children
and our hope
that travels through
our blood,
we would be
nothing more
than a physical
shell.
Even if you've never
learned it,
it is there
urging you forward,
pushing you harder
towards the future.
It is there
making you search
for what is lost.
It is there
building up resolve.
It is there
when you cry by yourself.
It is there
holding you up when you
crawl.
It is there.

A WORLD AT PEACE

A calm settled over the world and there was no more war, no more hunger, no more fear, no more sadness, no more racism, no more exhausting the land, no more hierarchy, no more greed, no more nuclear families or nuclear bombs, no more "I" and just "we," no more class systems, and no more desperation. This was the dream of the mother, holding her dying son in her arms on the Gaza Strip amidst the hysteria. This was the dream of the father who watched his family starve to death in a barren land, displaced from humanity. This was the dream of the brother who saw his sister give in to addiction because she lost hope and saw no way out. This was the dream of the sister who saw her brother off to war to fight in a battle she did not believe in and did not understand. This was the dream of the son who saw his parents die on the streets because of the class status they were born into. This was the dream of the First Nations who saw the land torn apart and pillaged until no life was left. This was the dream of the daughter who saw her mother fight her whole life just so that her children never had to suffer racism and hatred as much as she did. This was the dream of the grandfather who saw beauty dying and nothing left over for future generations to cherish. This was the dream of the grandmother who saw souls losing whatever hope was left and becoming desensitized to all the suffering in the world. This was the dream ...

INDIAN LOVE

I want to taste you
to love you
taste the sweat
feel the heat
feel you move
above me
beneath me
I want to
smell your lust
taste your musk
let it drip
down my lips
my chin
and tell you
I need you ...
But I just can't
suppress
Catholicism
that shackles my tongue ...

ONE IN THE SAME

I remember a place
separated by time
and generations,
where the fleeting
calls of the chickadee
echoed unabashed –

They knew their place.

Robust deer, young and old,
frolicked on the grassy skirts,
through the forests,
alongside banks of the meadows,
nibbling on earthy pastures,
resting in the cherry sun,
feeding their young
and man as well –

They knew their place.

Beavers worked, gnawed, and sliced
(the only clear-cutters I knew)
and fashioned circular abodes,
circles of life
for the cycle of life –

They knew their place.

At night,
when all was still,
except for the frog chatter,
one could hear the lonesome
cries of the wolf,
in steady contractions,
calling to his own –

He knew his place.

This place
is where Kokum knelt with great hardship
to arrange her love and respect
in the concretion of an offering.
Her gait weak from determination,
her breath laboured.
Life and breath
one in the same –
inhaling
breathing
inhaling
the unmistakable perfume
of Sweetgrass that grew
with unending purpose, poised,
tall, and waiting to be caressed,
and gathered with spirited, highered hands –

She knew her place.

And as I follow
in her very steps,
this place,
life, and breath
one in the same
in Mother Earth's courtyard,
I am humbled
by how short,
fragile,
and temporary
life is –

I know my place.

SOUTH

MOTHER EARTH'S SORROW

1

"I'm tired," said Mother Earth,
"of paying with my children's lives.
I'm tired of watching and waiting
for you to see what you have done to me.

"All my pure-white bears have
become hungry and rusty brown
from the metal monsters of the sea
that seem to litter the bottom of me.

"The fish have forgotten how to swim
and where to go! Years of interrupted travels
have made them lose their path!

"I'm dizzy and exhausted –
trying to keep my womb clean
and the knots out of my hair
that appear out of nowhere
every time you think of something new.

"Just wait and see!
When the trees are gone,
there will be no paper
to print your money on!
And as you stand and try
to make others believe
the unbelievable – but
you will not even listen! –
you have become
unplugged with your
greed to become the almighty.
You have become the
thunderstruck traveller!
And your stepping stones
have left blackened footprints
all over your own wings!

"You have become delirious
with your need for liftoff –
rooted in your selfishness!
Trap the beast of greed
that has been given the right over
the death of my children –
all backed into your corner,
right where you led them.
I called you all by name!
All your roadways, highways,
alleyways, and byways …
One road trip too many."

MOTHER EARTH'S SORROW

2

"My temperature is slowly rising
and **I** am weakened,
sick with fever –

"I feel my womb
compressing, shrinking,
older, and used … cornered.
I'm weary of watching my
children surrender their lives
unconsciously and without fight.

"I am a broken jigsaw
with my pieces tattered,
scattered, stained, and punctured.

"I'm tired of waiting for the obvious
awakening of
collective conscience and compassion …
I want to be taken care of
as I have taken care of you.
That is all it would take …"

LUNA

Can you hear her?
She calls out to her pod
on a moonless night;
mournful wails – haunting
the silent mountain faces,
climbing between each crack,
and staking silent claim.

I hear her calling and
I recognize that voice –
the voice of loneliness
clearing an empty space.

She strikes the breathing water
with her lustrous, merciless tail
and teardrops of the sea gently

multiply and fall,
descend with welcomed purpose
upon her great, bowed head,
and she knows she is alone.

Mist
across the mountain jags
sets its cold coverlet
amongst jagged faces.

To this night;
when you're all alone,
you can hear her cry
through the mist –
clotting the air with longing.

MOTHER THUNDER

I exist if only for the storms of Alberta
that saved me from a life of containment.
I knew without a doubt there was hope
after Mother Thunder shared her fire and her songs
and painted a picture beyond my yellowing past,
possessing me with poverty and circumstance.

I remember Mother Thunder's untrained beauty,
calling me as always from a time
before my eyes were open and clear
and my spirit was in denial
and my mind was locked.

I have not seen Mother Thunder
since I abandoned the Alberta plains
in a fight or flight to see and be more
than the confines of colonial walls.
The reservation does not call me home.
Wrapping around me tighter,
these colonial walls
smother me with memories.
But I am reminded of home when my
only friend was Mother Thunder.

I miss the crawling lightning
and the day-shattering moment
that reveals the stark of night striking light –
that is Mother Thunder's child called lightning,
who is my friend and calls to me from home,
who heightens, lightens, and brightens
the exact moment that the rain's fingertips
paint my face and I miss calling her name
and feeling her gentle anger ignite my fire.
Mother Thunder, who makes me dance in the rain,
stirs flashes of light across her cobalt canvas,
drenching me in her tears,
benches me in white light.
I miss the plains I have abandoned …

TWINKLE

TWINKLE

FALLEN

STAR

back in 1964,
mom tasted whisky
and it stained her lips –
a golden five-star brown.
she said it was the best
indian medicine around

i used to collect those golden stars ...
after all, mom told me ...
i could wish upon a star ...
and i wished my mom
would not collect those golden stars ...

i once slept in a teepee
with my golden stars
and stared out at the night,
praying and demanding god
or whoever i was
supposed to pray to,
wishing upon golden stars
to bring mom
back to me
back to my world
back from indian school ...

i asked god one day
why he was so cruel,
why he let a man of god
give my mom reason
to collect golden stars
to pass on to me ...

i ripped off the golden stars
the teacher so happily placed
upon my white papers ...

RED LIES

I've been lying since I was 7
when I knew there was no heaven
when hell was lying next to me –
how easy it was to lie.
Being poor and all
they'd pour straight off my lips –

I picked through cast-off clothing
choosing faded pinks, dead reds
from the thrift store's garbage
Trying to start trends
10 years too late –

Oh and Mommy and Daddy
were waiting at home
with a cake
with my name
excruciatingly,
painstakingly,
written in pink
swirly-cue peaks
just for me …
Oh how the boys and girls
gathered near
just to hear
just how sweet
and what a treat
(just mine and only mine)

the swirly-cue mountain
so blessed and prominent
that was my name
standing pretty
surrounded by white –

Oh how tremendous
and powerful
and free
when I changed my name
to escape the shame
and decided to hide,
thumbed a ride –

How un-Indian I felt
and wanted to be
the day my Indian locks
fell to the white floor
and the roots were tortured
a burnt-honey blonde –

Oh how preciously pure
I felt when I said,
"You were the first,"
because obviously
by some twisted,
unpredictable,
colonization disease,

set years ago,
did I lose my innocence –
But in my mind,
you were the first.
And I'll forever stand by this
red lie
because obviously by
some trap and truth
there could only be
lies
spinning about
like flies –
Oh how brave
and courageous I felt
to finally tell
that, all of it,
all of me.
I lied
to save myself
from your lies …

THIS MOMENT TOO SHALL PASS

I want to see
your eyes sparkle
with the love
you feel for me
and have you gently
push aside the stray tendrils
that seem to fall
at the right or wrong moment
as we momentarily look away
to gaze off into the
empty
space
above
hushing sea.

That gentle toss of your head.
In reality, you're scared
as you engulf my hand
and tell me of the time
you fell out of a tree.
And now I stare at the
crescent-shaped scar
that highlights your leg
and wish I could have
been there
to catch you.
It's just the newness
as I find myself smiling,
replaying in my mind's
picture show
events of the day
and moments
I want to relive.
"It's better to have loved."

THIS MOMENT TOO SHALL PASS

So as I lie here,
slowly tracing
your face
while you
hold me in your arms,
I become fragile
from the gentleness
of your voice
made raspy
by your need
that I am afraid to lose.

Everything I have ever
loved
has passed
just like this moment
as I trace your face,
watch you breathe,
and feel our daughter
kick from within ...

THE HIGHWAY OF FEARS

My mother wove herself into my mind,
through my heart
my vision
my grief
For once I let it all go. I knew she loved me
just like all the other Indian children
abandoned
taken
forsaken
objectified
We were all loved by broken spirits
in the middle of broken times.

Their lives riddled with
disconnectedness
shame
distrust
self-hatred
self-blame
physical abuse
mental abuse
sexual abuse
emotional abuse
spiritual abuse

The past
the present
the future
became anything
but absolute.

I felt something
pure and good
kicking
hoping
believing
growing
merging
inside me
where sorrow
could not reach.

I was afraid, in love,
entranced by our bond

never

meant to be broken.
Time and time again,
the bond was broken
in my ancestors' lives,
even as close to me as my
own mother, who had to let go
of her fears. Her past would
have eaten me alive and no one
would have noticed the little Indian
girl gone missing in a sea of grey misery.
The highway of tears confirms this ...

I want to hold my daughter,
touch her black hair.
I cannot let go,
do not want to let go,
but I understand why
my mother did.

I understand why
a lot of mothers
let go.

I feel just how vulnerable
I once was in the arms
of a
broken
doll.
So, lost and alone, dysfunctional,
she knew in her heart that in that
time she could not protect
that vulnerability no matter how much
she wanted to ...
I want for my daughter swimming in maternal
waters to know that there is good in the world.
I never want her to get lost and wonder of her existence.
I want her to see me mend my broken fences of the past.
Me and her

WEST

THE GAZA STRIPPED

We will never see the sunrise the same way someone
else not of war sees it when it rises east and dances west –
There is no time to reflect on the conception of a new day
and what beauty can blossom – when surrounded by carnage,
waiting to either succumb or prevail, another day eating
our provisions and flower petals as we contemplate this
and wonder how we ever ended up eating the same diet
as our animals who are less of a threat to our impending demise –
it is not a thought that enters their minds as they chew
on flower petals, stems, and pollen'ous' carnations.

We wonder if we even have a purpose and, if so,
what it could possibly be as we hide and steal away
searching for food in barren fields of dry bounty,
dying and withering away in the mid-morning sun.

Could creation use humanity to teach others lessons?
And if that is so, how is one chosen to endure persistent fear,
loved ones lost, hunger and hopelessness living in chants and chains?
As I gather my bug-eaten, shrunken wheat – reciting words of
possible redemption and the prevalence of good,
silently begging the Creator and sending positive energy out into the
universe,
hoping to be spared so I may possibly make an ounce of difference
for those who have lost their loved ones, their lives,
for those who have lost hope, have stopped dreaming
because, after dreaming ten thousand dreams of relief,
nothing has changed but the calendar date no one wants
to keep track of as the days go by, repeating,
"I can feel the hatred in their hearts" as they stare
down at us, hating the very idea that we were born,
loathing the thought of our courage and will to tread
and still want a full belly before we lie down in exhaustion.
And we pray for the people who want to protect us
for, if they don't survive, then we don't have
even a tiny seed of hope to plant in our children's minds.

What good is a seed of hope if there is nowhere to plant it,
no one to watch over it, to feed it, to care if it grows.

I let out another deep sigh I have been holding,
clasping together my very own hands that can do
no more than furiously grasp each other and yet
gently hold a dying loved one or a dying stranger,
tears falling and getting lost in why it wasn't me
lying on the dusty shell-littered ground, finally free
from the persecution of ideas, hatred, and living in fear,
wishing and wanting death to call my very own name
if it meant my passing could save humanity from the
very same with the same coloured blood and the ability
to love another and want to reproduce
and pass on that love and have a piece of us
carrying the future on by sanity or insanity
depending on which side you were born.

These two hands cannot stop the rising death toll.
I kneel down, two hands on my head, begging
for my loved ones to see another sky of diamond
and to hold on just a little longer … Doesn't goodness
always prevail even in the face of enormous suffering?
Life continues and new hopes are born, I want to believe,
I have to believe, and perhaps one day I will wake up
and be thankful to see the sun and feel it on my skin
without impending threat, and the light and warmth
gracing and grazing my face and these two praying hands,
have not felt the sun's impression for the last encounter.

These two eyes of mine are waiting to adjust to night,
falling when the darkness covers us in peace and silence –
Even the men filled with anger, cold hatred, loaded guns,
two eyes, and two hands have to sleep sometime.

If only they could see what I see, feel what I feel,
hope what I hope, and just stop for a minute
to see human suffering as a catalyst that can bring
about change and persecuted death as a means
to question why human sorrow, human loss, and

killing in cold blood could ever be called anything
but imbalanced perspective in the form of violence,
blood flowing down the streets, congealing in dust pools.
The very thought of a Creator coveting hatred to fester and multiply,
divide, fall, and become absolute, or cause his children to
kill or maim another in cold blood, actually feeling that
death all along was the only solution to divided thoughts,
with hatred strewn about and boiled in their minds,
entrenched in false righteousness as if anyone could be
right in the biggest sin of all, judging me and sealing my fate,
pushing position without permission and unbalancing
the true laws of Mother Nature.

The cover of night slinks in like an expected guest
and the stars appear before me on black canvas,
and I know I have lived another day in chants and chains,
redemption and sorrow, love and hatred,
fear and reverence, begging for reprieve.
I will never be a doctor and watch new life unfold,
wishing I was not born of suffering on the Gaza Strip.
I will never see my mother and father smile for
the coming morn when the sun plants itself outside our door.
My mother has never tilled and planted a garden without
threat of either gunfire or the hunger of her family
piercing her heart, soul, courage, and the will to go on
for just one more day, she whispers as she wipes her brow.
She has never planted a single rose and had the privilege
to watch it bud and flower new hope and peace, pushing
forth in the brilliance of a peaceful sunrise.

The flowers in bloom are to be fed to the animals
and perhaps to our children and mothers as well.

I have never had the chance to see her smile in the sun
without worry and sorrow, hoping this day is the day
her loved ones are spared their lives or, at the very least,
a quick and painless death with the light of goodness
and truth written on our faces as we succumb to
their ideology of
conclusion.

COLONIAL PEST-ASIDE

Trails of spoiled
cultures, beliefs
across the canvas, span
generations penetrated.
Fragmented,
pushed aside on
divided lands
by divided minds

Colonial pesticide

Scared into submission,
battles of un-GOD-ly conflict
dripping with clotting crimson
fiery damnation

Book of domination
teaching rules of shame
and pre-eminent position

Frozen, salty tears
eroding, rusting;
gnarled, broken dolls,
hearts hanging
over the hearth,
muted tongues,
force-fed
flaming words of righteousness,
sharp, penetrating into flesh
threatened fiery pits of hell

Damning, dividing
into defeated, manageable
masses of broken spirits.

False teachings
false understandings
false sense of identity

Colonial pesticide

TORN IN THREE

Was never meant to be
the success of us three
set by a fate not ours
by nuns' and priests' power –
Who gave them that power?
If not my very own Creator,
who allows us to be humble
and allows us the pleasure of
tasting life with the fruitful
tongues of passion
and love of thyself …

'Twas in the church where I tasted
the sinful richness of red wine,
the very same wine that swallowed
my mother whole and spit out her soul.
"In moderation," just a recommendation
for those who have not travelled
on the lonely road of geno-sui-cide,
frozen in the minds and spirits of
our very own mothers, grandmothers,
fathers, grandfathers, sisters, brothers,
uncles, aunts, and our children …

Just who or what was to become of us
as original dwellers of this so-called North America –
never dawned on anyone that we would need answers
to questions brought on by years of a-cultural lag,
trying to keep up with technology because resources
disappeared just as soon as they were of some use
no matter how insignificant it seemed in Mother
Nature's bigger picture of an unspoken agreement
to honour her children, her animals, her creations;
another promise broken, another treaty made ...

Eventually we learned a biased history
of the savages, the hated, the romanticized, the hero,
the last one standing on the corner with tears staining
our tired faces looking upwards – still battling the same
battle – this time with words from the law that also promised
to take care of its inhabitants – the queen's wards
forgotten about, talked about, tossed about ...

Upwards – always looking upwards – because we were
too tired to look down at the ground that has seen
so many Indian bones buried by the queen's men.
Our queens were our mothers, our grandmothers, our sisters,
our aunts, our daughters, our nieces, ourselves –

ELUSIVE INDIAN CREATURES

I am the elusive Indian creature
Alone and unfulfilled, sought-after and feared.
Fearful of the selfish scavenger exploits –
Trembling in my sunken museum teepee,
Praying in the harsh cold of raven night
Family scattered like dandelion tufts
Landing in stale, earthless concrete
Forever trying to blend in yet hide
Not wanting to be found – I know the truth
And still have to clasp my lips shut tight,
no one believes in Indian creatures anymore …

ARTEFACTS

Artefacts
of lost love
Capture my space
Invade my tired heart and
detain my restive soul... picture of a
dead husband much loved yet abandoned in a
time when inward anguish swallowed him – love, soul,
mind – and gone was Daddy in a sea of heroin. Black dresses, fancy
underwear, and glass wastebaskets, oil paintings, pastel sketches, love cards,
tarot cards, glass shards unrequited, unaware, unrealistic, unresolved ... the undoing
of it all. Dust settles in silence all around me as my heart aches for one day in the past when love
didn't have to hurt and daddies didn't do drugs and mommies weren't recovering from sexual
abuse and skin colour was rain, rain, and more rain indistinguishable from other rain
spilling onto the cold, wet ground with fervour and fever and a want for all
blood to be red when it spills and tastes the same, none sweeter, nor
saltier, none redder than the next gutted raindrop in a sea
of cold, wet pavement where compassion should
reside ... on the cold pavement beside
a puddle of rain, pictures of
dead husbands and
heroin.

FORGIVENESS

How do you piece together a nation
tormented ... fragmented ... residual?
Always blindly reaching for the stars,
racing against time, people, and place,
never quite catching or measuring up,
and never quite maintaining
nor reclaiming equality in the true
sense as stated in the Charter of
Rights and Freedoms?
I call it ...
Charter of Rights and fairy tales;
tried, denied, and Disney-fied.

Always searching blindly
like a child reaching for her
mother in the dark.
Never really knowing if she's
really there ... but just believing.

I once sat amongst fallen stars
so tired of reaching blindly
that they gave up in their minds,
their souls, and their hearts.
I listened to their voices tremble
and spit out the truth in another mother
tongue; just not their own mother
silenced.

I heard the word "forgiveness"
and I asked in what language
does it really begin?

An achievement of peace – finally
painted the colour of forgiveness
shape-shifted their faces,
showing a different time
of acceptance, love, peace,
and a place to finally rest;
way before it was their time.
But I understood.

Then I watched a thing of beauty.
It really is for my people whose
wounds could just not heal.
Maybe there wasn't enough time?
Maybe too much time?
Or maybe in their calm – but tragic – deaths
we can really only understand
what it has meant for so many years,
decades, centuries, what it meant,
and what it still means to be Indian.
Understanding is one thing ...
forgiveness is another.

PSALM BILL C-31

The colonists reigneth
clothed in materialism:
clothed in self-indulgence,
wherewith he hath exalted himself:
the world is under destruction,
and it cannot be saved.
Thy thoughts thriving of past,
Thou importance from surpassing.
The quakes have begun.
Oh colonists, the deaths have exposed reality:
The quakes and floods honour thy mother.
The colonists are more vociferous than the truths,
yea, than the mighty quakes in the Ring of Fire.
Thy falsehoods set in books of stone:
Selfishness becometh thine death –

NORTH

COLLECTIVE TEARS OF UNITY

When

love spreads

its encompassing

wings across the impatience

of our searching hearts – we are but

single souls waiting for our twins in the starless

darkness of this very night – Afraid of the clutches of jealousy

and greed to evoke another ecological loss never to be recovered

at least in this precious lifetime we apparently have chosen to live and

have promised change. Small single souls trying to conceive the realities humanity

has so far managed to abandon with each dulling technological suffocation and the tears

are frozen and our minds wander to other places where the pain of war, hunger, poverty,

and the devastation of love do not exist in the mortal sense but lay assertion to the collective

conscience of harmony uniting and bringing together one collective mind with no fear – only love,

acceptance, and compassion for the weak hearted and the weak minded forever searching for the

forgiveness of time, willing it to stop just long enough to catch up with the spiritual world that

slowly loses light with each and every unused moment – It is the only thing that is real and

the only thing to hang on to with a passion to live as our Mother Earth succumbs

to the loss of her womanhood and her ability

to replenish herself.

ONE THOUSAND CRANES

Someone set sail one thousand cranes
last night in the spirit world of amethyst dreams.
Someone wished the sun to kiss your cheeks
and opalescent moonbeams to paint
light in the darkness so you never lose your way.

Someone dreamt of a painted sea turtle
last night who knew one thousand secrets,
who was the keeper of the doorway to the
spirit world that sits on the ocean's edge – he said.

Someone wished for you last night
an orchard of cherry blossoms
dancing gracefully in the wind,
reminding you to be gentle and kind
to yourself and never forget
to dance in the wind as cherry blossoms
soar in warm winds, dance with them,
just be and remember me – they said.

Someone dreamt of you in the spirit world
last night in a valley of fuchsia baby azaleas
and a white camellia in your hair
reminding you to patiently wait for the
sea turtles' secrets at the edge of the ocean.

Someone wished for you last night
one thousand cranes to guide you to them
in the twilight and astral of your sleep –

They say when sorrow is too great
they do not want to come too soon
for you may never want to leave
the dream world – and so they wait
at the edge of your dreams with love
resonating, encompassing you, for love
has no timeline and reaches beyond
the edges of the human sorrow.

Someone whispered to you last night,
you will dream of them on a white
Manchurian crane when you are ready
to let their essence into the light
and finally smile when you think of them.
Place bluebells in the lightest room
to remind you of how grateful
they were to know you and love you.
Place lavender under your pillow
for tender dreams where loved ones meet.
And we will fold one thousand cranes
in a field of flowering sweet-pea flowers
and budding zinnia, and we will let soar
one thousand cranes over a thousand dreams
above our temporary goodbye,
and we will have wished someone else
peace, love, strength, light in the darkness –
And one thousand cranes …

CHAI TEA RANT

Last night I went for a drive for about two hours. I thought I better before the gas prices go up again, so I put in the last $10 bill I had in my wallet and away I went driving over the bridge, under the bridge, around the bridge, around the other bridge, under the other bridge, Ambleside, Tim Hortons with my $1.64 and said to myself, "Hell yeah! I'm at least worth a large chai tea." All the while playing a CD I made and titled "Babe's Sad Songs." (I figured I may as well be someone's babe, yeah, someone's babe … my own …) I listened to all these songs that I so carefully or carelessly put together, depending on whatever purpose there was supposed to be. I sang along to John Waite's "I ain't missing you at all," and out came the tears of sadness and anger and thoughts of friends, family, both here physically and those here only in spirit. Then I wasn't angry anymore; only sad to realize that my parents weren't able to protect me from sexual abuse. In the next song, Shania Twain sang, "Black eyes … / Blue tears give me freedom." Then I missed my mom and dad and was also very angry that they did not protect me when they couldn't even protect themselves. Then Sheryl Crowe and the Dixie Chicks sang "Would you be man enough to be my man?" and all my thoughts went to all the failed, broken, hurtful relationships. I thought of all the lessons learned with one-on-one individualized relationship deconstruction and figured there ain't no better lesson than men in the raw. I thought of the good times with the relationships as well and laughed and marvelled at different strategies and how we tried to control each other. The song after that was R.E.M.'s "Everybody Hurts" and I cried and as the tears blurred my view of the road and, as I veered back into my own lane, I thought about my dad's funeral – this was the song he wanted played at his funeral. He used to play it in his counselling sessions to get people to open up. A recovering alcoholic, he kept saying it, even after he quit close to twenty-five years or so. I understood because sometimes I just want to go off the deep end like my mother with a wine bottle in every pocket; staining my small little mouth a deep, almost dried blood-coloured red. Then I think that I'd only have to pick myself up at the bottom of the gutter and trek back up and face my harshest critic in the mirror once again and this time I would have lost my purse, knocked out my smoke-stained abused teeth, found a psychic healer's card in my bra, called all the people on my cell call list and told them I loved them, getting my phone cut off in the process – then I would have pulled out my $1.64 and got a chai tea by walking through the drive thru … And thought to myself, "I must be still worth $1.64 …"

POW WOW DREAMS

Oh little one
With the beautiful bustle
You are so at peace, I feel it
Did your momma take the time
and energy she wished was
taken with her; and watch your
eyes dance at the sight of your outfit?
Did she colour her future with colours
She prayed about and chose just for you?
Did she take out her camera and draw
so near, and permanently make a memory
of you whom she dances for in dreams?
Did she finally stop having nightmares
of what she had lost so long ago?
Living through you to set her free?
The confident steps, the liquid movements,
And the proud sweat never left your face
As you gently wove moccasin footprints
Upon Mother Earth's beauty in the sun.

Oh golden age, proud women
with aged grace, and painful milestones
weaving tales with gentle lines around
your secret smile and sparkling eyes,
Are you happy the day is here?
That the little ones are unashamed
Following in your footsteps?

Oh elders with your headpieces,
Your eagle feathers and staff;
It is breathtaking after all the trials;
that you stand before us
with pain etched upon your faces
like a picture for all to see and remember.

Do you see the smiles all around
as you solidly keep the circle closed and strong?
Just by living in your moment and sharing it too?
Do you see it in the depths of your peoples' souls?

Oh little one with the jingle dress
so bright and beautiful. Wind chimes echo
with each and every proud, enchanting tiptoe,
mesmerizing, bringing back the time of freedom
and shadows by an open fire telling of days gone?
Do you see just what you do to me?

It is so hard not to cry as I see
Being Indian shouldn't have had to hurt ...
I only wish our mothers and grandmothers
And our great-grandmothers were here
To see and feel what they dreamt of ...

STANDING ON THIN ICE

The young polar bear
stood on thin ice,
scanning the horizon,
her pregnant belly empty –
Her nose twitched and tested the air
for any sign of life she might try and take.
A lone seal, seemingly lost, bobbed
and mewed as the night grew around her.
They were both ready to give up –
one from hunger and the other from loneliness –
seal pup lost in the sea and polar mother on the shore,
watching each other's eyes, sensing each other's
dilemma; waiting for what? They did not know
the baby seal did not know how to hope
and the empty, rusty-tinged mother did not know
how to hunt; her own mother gone ...
The ice melted way too fast.
The baby seal's eyes fogged over
near death, lacking any motivation
to bob and wait for a miracle –
deep down in her own ocean.
She felt at one with the sea
just as she always did.
Except, this time, she was alone.
She did not know death,
but she saw it and still did not understand.
That is why she was unafraid. She only knew
the small alcove where she fell from her mother
and into the rising temperature of the sea.
She looked in her mother's eyes as she
dropped her head to the slush with
a soft crunch that not even the polar bear

could hear. The fish left early that year
and some never arrived or journeyed through,
for the huge metal monsters of the sea
ate them all, and baby seal's mother died.
And now being only four days old
and having not suckled in three days,
she drank small amounts of the sea
and chewed on the ice the first and second day.

The third day, she bobbed and did not realize
she was even waiting. She dragged her down-
kissed body upon the shore of the dying iceberg
And huffed and sighed and settled as best she could,
for she was too tired of nothing much.
She was so little and young and did not know
to sense anything but hunger and exhaustion.
She lay down next to her mother who had become
icy and still and watched as the rusty-white blur
approached; she did not shrink in fear or back
up to plunge into her birthplace.
She huffed once more, sending swirling tufts
of her scent into the air and succumbed to hunger
just before soon-to-be mother bear approached.
Lucky for her, this day, this year, the ice
was melting faster and the fish
did not come, for she did not know how
to hunt. She was a foraging
polar bear, belly heavily sagging,
breathing almost meditatively. She fell asleep.
And the shore she slept on broke off
And the swelling, inexperienced swimmer
floated off into the warm, starry night …

ALCOHOL

I can be your
best friend
when things
go wrong and
you want to run.
I am so available
for the price of a song.
I will be by your side as long
as you reach for me with open arms.
I don't care what you look like or if you
act like a fool; I can be there day or night
at your beck and call. With you I will not fight.
I will never leave you alone until the time is right.
I can colour any situation any colour that you choose;
I can colour your past and paint your future, take your
life; hold you in my hands; mask your pain and never
ever let you go. It's up to you but in the end you will lose.
I can be your friend; your one and only friend or I can be
your enemy and lead you to death's door quick and painful.
Just remember, I will never leave you if you choose to stay.
I will never leave you but you must know; your family may.
They can't take the pressure that I've got you by the hand.
Just don't love me too much cuz, when I get a hold of you,
my clutches start to tear your life apart; I do not fight fair
and I really don't care, the door to leave is always there

Remember I am not fair;
When you fall in love with
me. You know who I am
You know all about
me
and
it's
all
up to you … I am **alcohol**

IN THE DOG HOUSE

Teardrops hang from barren trees,
sickly grass slouches upon the
earthly bed –
defeated,
disassociated.

Cold, washed-out blue,
flanked by threatening billows,
encircling and encasing the dog house
and two lives buried within it.

She hunches in fetal pose
in the back of the dog house.
She counts spiral knotholes,
seizing her breath,
tracing nature's patterns,
now forced to be a part
of something else

her something else –
her somewhere else
she'd rather be.

She traces the knotholes
and counts them over and over again
and feels a false consolation.
"Yes," she says to herself, "still 7."

Indifferent splats of rain
rap on the weather-battered roof.
Thin arms embrace shivering dog.
Listening for footsteps,
she hopes they are
rain beats
or heartbeats,
and not footsteps.

Bone-cold water
oozes through the cracks,
trickling, seeking end.
She can hear the dog's life drum
as weary as her own.
Finally,
her lost breath returns.
They both fall asleep

In the safety of the dog house.

ACKNOWLEDGEMENTS

This book is dedicated to numerous First Nations people like my mother, who until today did not have a voice;

to my father, who kept pushing me forward no matter where I was in life;

to my brother J.J., who was always my best friend throughout my life, who knows me so well, and who helped me remember my father's teachings of the medicine wheel;

to my brother Hank, who continues to keep me thinking;

to Joanne Arnott for being a great friend both on the patio with a coffee and in the classroom with writing tools and thinking caps;

to Victor J. for helping me achieve my educational goals;

to Roberta JXYZ, the healing angel sent to me from above to make me laugh and cry, sometimes within the same minute and same sentence;

to Ian Perry, who never knew what an impact his teaching and his warm heart had on me and many other children;

to my uncles Gabe and Charlie;

to Grace Woo, who never stopped believing in me and who in turn wrote an academic book after I told her to help "us" (meaning First Nations people);

to Brenda J., who was my second mother growing up;

to Lee Davidson, who at times held my pitiful medicine wheel (strapped together with duct tape) and who continues to be the voice of my guardian angel and of reason;

to Michelle S. for supporting me through thick and thin;

to Karen B. for your support and many hours spent talking about what is important;

to Amber and Jamie for always being real and making me feel like home is anywhere;

to Carol T., Vonnie B., and Donna B., wherever you are in the world;

to Jerry Saddleback for bringing me closer to myself and to Mother Earth

and for answering questions about the medicine wheel;
to Gary A-Z for teaching me the value of life through struggle and thoughts and for doing all those funny impressions of people;
to GTM and his mother, Phyllis, for seeing something and believing in my work and making it possible to share my truth;
to Kevin Williams, Greg Gibson, Ann-Marie Metten, and Les Smith at Talonbooks;
to the Canada Council for the Arts for a grant under the Aboriginal Writers, Storytellers, and Publishers Grant program that aided in the writing of these poems;
and, last but not least, to my reasons for living – my children – who have taught me so much, who continue to shine and teach me about life, and who inspire me with their smiles and silliness meant only for mama.

Special thanks to the editors of journals or organizers of events where some of these poems were previously published or read:

"Mother Earth's Sorrow 1 and 2" was inspired by the art piece titled *Armchair Traveller* during Hosted, an art and poetry collaboration event featuring Pandora's Collective poets, the Word Whips Writing Series, and the artwork of Assia Linkovsky

"Luna" and "Red Lies" also appeared in the Aboriginal Writers Collective West Coast's *Salish Seas Anthology*

"In the Dog House" was previously published in *Quills Canadian Poetry*

"One Thousand Cranes" appeared in the program of the Ganbare Japan! benefit concert, held Tuesday, April 19, 2011, at Vancouver's Queen Elizabeth Theatre to help the people of Japan following the Tohoku earthquake and tsunami.

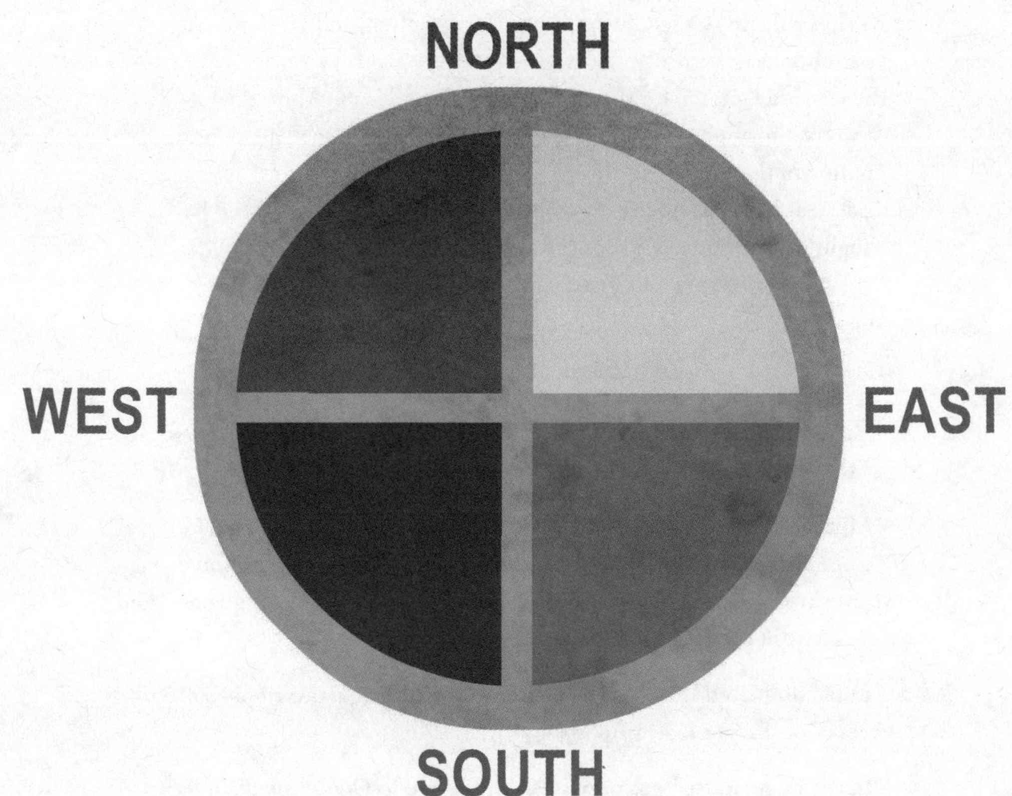
NORTH
WEST
EAST
SOUTH

THE MEDICINE WHEEL

When I was fourteen years old, I left the reserve in Alberta and, by age nineteen, I was on my way to Vancouver, pregnant, naive, and full of hope for the baby growing in my womb and about to change my life. I wanted to protect the new being who somehow chose me to be her mama. I heard somewhere that we choose our parents and maybe in fact we do. At first, we may not always understand why, but we do understand someday.

Several years later, my father sat me down and with felt markers and two poster boards proceeded to explain the teachings of the medicine wheel. My father seemed to need to explain all this to me even though I wasn't ready to listen. By that time – twenty-one years ago now – I had immersed myself in the Vietnamese culture and was not prepared to listen to stories from my past. Nevertheless, my father had travelled to the coast to see me and I respected him enough to sit still and hear him out. Most of what I am going to say here are my recollections from that day, when I listened with half an ear yet with love and respect for my father as an elder of our community. I still remember how he looked in his burgundy shirt and black dress pants as my two half-Asian children jumped on his lap, clamouring for his attention. I wish I still had the two poster boards he made; unfortunately, these sacred teachings from my father about the trials and lessons of the world were lost in a fire.

Twenty-one years ago, when my father told me about the medicine wheel, I remember that on one poster board, he drew a timeline and, on the other, a medicine wheel. On the timeline, he drew a thick line establishing first contact and then proceeded to mark dates that changed the "Indian" way of life forever. He marked 1862, when smallpox swept the land, killing nearly one in every three First Nations in British Columbia. He marked 1871 to 1881, when the transcontinental railroad was built and still no one wanted to hire an Indian. He marked 1954, when Prohibition was lifted and First Nations were allowed to drink in public places. He talked about residential schools opening up in the mid- to late 1800s; the forced sterilization of Native women in Alberta between 1929 and 1972; the Sixties Scoop, which began in the 1960s and continued into the late 1980s, when many First Nations children were apprehended and fostered or adopted, usually into White families. He talked about the fur trade and First Nations economies changing from bartering to money. He talked about how many Aboriginal people were ashamed to be First Nations because they didn't understand what had happened to them. He talked about loss of culture, traditions, way of life, way of thinking, language, and even child-rearing methods.

On the second poster board, my father took his time to draw a huge, perfect circle that he divided into four parts; then he asked me if I knew what it was. I said it was a circle. He looked at me for a minute and said it was more than a circle; it was a way of life and it held the whole world inside it. He explained that the medicine wheel has four parts because it holds many things. It holds the four aspects of the self: physical, mental, spiritual, and emotional. It holds all races of people, whom we must respect regardless of colour or belief. It holds the four seasons, every plant and tree, and all four-legged and two-legged animals. My father told me everyone and everything has a place within this circle and that it is the cycle of all life. For humans, he said that the medicine wheel represents the four stages of life we go through while living on this earth. First, we are babies needing every aspect of our being to be cared for; then we are youths; then we become adults; and then we come full circle again as elders who one day will need to be cared for as we once were cared for as babies. The four elements earth, air, fire, and water are also a part of this circle and we must care for these elements as well: they are gifts, not commodities. My father explained how colonization had affected "Indian" people and that we need to follow the medicine wheel to regain ourselves: one aspect of the medicine wheel must not be out of balance or they all become out of balance.

My father, "Herman" John, a.k.a. John Kehewin, was a great man, who tried to live his life in balance according to the medicine wheel, without focusing too much on any one aspect of the "self." He taught me that crying is a gift and that forgiveness is very important to finding balance in life. He taught me to see past the pain to find where it first began. My father was a man of his word, a lover of "his" people, a strong believer in keeping the family together, a role model, and definitely a character. He and his best friend – his cousin Robert – would dress up as an old married couple every Halloween and dance together at sober dances. My father was a traveller on the "Red Road," who believed in sobriety as a way of life. His work in the Kehewin community, as well as at the Manawanis Native Friendship Centre in St. Paul, Alberta, helped many people and families come to terms with the past. He prayed every night for everyone he could think of. He prayed for the world. Even though I left many years ago, back home I am not known as Wanda; instead, I've come to be known as "Herman's daughter," which is as good an introduction as any.

When my father told me about the medicine wheel, he talked about trying to restore balance within the self in order to help yourself and perhaps the people around you. He told me to go back to school and learn about history and that, one day when I understood, I would come home. I tried not to roll my eyes but he caught me and said, "What I am telling you today, you will remember and, my girl, you will come home." I argued with him and I told him I would never go home to a place that was hopeless and that caused so much pain and struggle. He argued back that one day I would be proud to be "Indian" and I would teach my children about being Indian. The problem is that it is quite a task to teach things to my children when a way of life and thinking is gone. So here I sit searching online and phoning near and far, looking for concrete answers about the teachings of the medicine wheel. The conclusion is that there are many different teachings but this is what I remember from my father.

As I try to reconstruct the past with contemporary tools, I remember my father and his love for his work within the First Nations communities and how the teachings of balance from the medicine wheel have inspired me to hang on to what is lost and to process what is found. It is a reminder that nothing lasts forever and we must record history in as unbiased a way as possible. I guess what my father meant by "coming home" was that one day I would come back both to my culture and to myself. The hardest part about this journey and the reclamation of the self is trying to piece together traditions and culture from bits of information from numerous sources. It is like trying to finish a jigsaw puzzle not knowing how many pieces are needed or what the picture is supposed to be.

Using the sacred teachings I remember from my father and from conversations with my family, I have organized the poems in *In the Dog House* according to the four aspects of the medicine wheel. I have organized the poems to balance the physical, the mental, the emotional, and the spiritual aspects of life and of the medicine wheel.

The physical aspect is represented in the east. The sun rises in the east, bringing new life and warmth; hence, birth and childhood are in this section. The physical aspect represents the Asian race. The element of air resides in this quadrant.

The mental aspect is represented in the south. It is the time of summer and love, but also the time of adolescence and continuous movement. The mental aspect represents the Red Nation. Here the element of earth resides.

The emotional aspect is represented in the west. This is the time of adulthood and responsibility and a time to connect with our children, who teach us to get up when we fall. The emotional aspect represents the Black race. The element of fire resides here.

The spiritual aspect is represented in the north. As elders, we turn back into children who need help in daily life. The spiritual aspect represents the White nation and winter, a time for deep introspection and personal growth. Here the element of water resides.

These aspects start in the east and end in the north and, together, they form the circle of life – a tradition of balance that my father shared with me and that I now share with you.

Wanda John-Kehewin has studied criminology, sociology, and Aboriginal studies with the Native Education Centre, Langara College, and Douglas College and creative writing with Simon Fraser University's The Writers' Studio. Wanda John uses writing as a therapeutic medium to understand and respond to the near decimation of First Nations culture, language, and tradition. She has been published in *Quills Canadian Poetry*, Aboriginal Writers Collective West Coast's *Salish Seas Anthology*, University of British Columbia's anthology of Aboriginal writing, *Alberta Sweetgrass*, *Ricepaper*, and Simon Fraser University's *emerge* anthology. She has shared her writing on "Wax Poetic" and "World Poetry Café," broadcast over Vancouver Co-op Radio, and has read at numerous events throughout the Lower Mainland, including those organized by the Writers' Union of Canada. Wanda John was awarded the 2013 World Poetry Empowered Poet Award and more of her work can be found on the *worldpoetry.ca* website.